I0068243

The Confident, Inspired Woman

Leadership Series

Book 1

DESIGN YOUR CULTURE EMPOWER YOUR TEAM

The Proven 5-Step Process

By Donna K Woolam

2014 Edition
Copyright © 2014 by Donna K Woolam

The information contained within this book is the opinion of the author only, and is not meant to diagnose, treat nor endorse any particular treatment for mental health issues. The author is not a doctor nor clinician. Any perceived promises of financial increase is purely accidental. The author does not make promises as to the effectiveness of this program other than the statement that the process has been proven to work in her experience and realm of influence.

Comments, Questions or Suggestions?
All feedback welcomed at Donna@DonnaWoolam.com
Publisher: Living At My Best – http://livingatmybest.com
Author: http://donnawoolam.com

A Personal Word from Donna

The power to transform the lives of people is within the hands of every person. It doesn't take a special gift, it simply takes a desire to make a difference.

I believe that YOU are such a person. Why do I believe this? Because YOU have chosen to purchase a book and download additional resources that will enable you to change a culture from one thing to another. That change will transform the lives of the people you influence from this day onward.

I was influenced by many people, but one particular woman led many by example. Her name is Kim Lipe. I met Kim during my years in the Direct Sales industry. She was, and is, a hardworking woman; passionate about her family, and the women she leads. Kim didn't set herself up to be an influence, she simply is.

During a challenging time in my career, she took the time to speak with me about what makes leaders great. I wasn't part of her group, she had nothing to gain from my success, but she gave me her time and wisdom any way.

I'm blessed to have had many women mentors throughout my life; in the church, in the traditional workplace, and in non-traditional workplace environments.

My encouragement to you today is this, learn all that you can and pass that knowledge on to others. Some will soar, some will not. Some will follow, some will not. Those decisions are not up to you. The results are not up to you. The only thing that is up to you, is to do your part.

I pray that as you work through these resources that you will learn more from them than you even imagined.

As always,

Live Inspired – Live at Your Best

Donna

Contents

INTENTION   7

4 Factors (4 "I's") 7

Basic Values Worksheet 8

Craft Your Vision Statement Worksheet 11

In the space below, write out your completed Vision Statement. 11

Craft Your Mission Statement Worksheet 12

Target Goal Setting Worksheet 13

SMART Target Goals Worksheet 14

Specific | Measurable | Action-Oriented | Realistic | Time Bound 14

INFORMATION   15

Information Flow Chart 15

INTERACTION   16

Basic Group Meeting Agenda 16

Agenda Items 16

Topic 16

Presenter 16

Time allotted 16

OTHER INFORMATION 16

INFLUENCE   17

Influence Your World Worksheet 17

INTERRUPTION   18

Interruption Worksheet 18

IMPLEMENTATION 20

Declaration of Worth 20

W.O.W. Cards (Within One Week) 21

Last Thoughts   22

What Next?   23

Connect With Donna 25

Other Books by Donna K Woolam 25

INTENTION   7

    4 Factors (4 "I's") 7

    Basic Values Worksheet 8

    Craft Your Vision Statement Worksheet 11

    Craft Your Mission Statement Worksheet 12

    Target Goal Setting Worksheet 13

    SMART Target Goals Worksheet 14

INFORMATION 15

    Information Flow Chart 15

INTERACTION   16

Basic Group Meeting Agenda 16

INFLUENCE   17

    Influence Your World Worksheet 17

INTERRUPTION 18

    Interruption Worksheet 18

IMPLEMENTATION 20

    Declaration of Worth 20

    W.O.W. Cards (Within One Week) 21

Last Thoughts   22

What Next?   23

Connect With Donna 25

    Other Books by Donna K Woolam 25

INTENTION

The first step in Designing Culture is defining the Intention of your organization. These resources are designed to equip you in this process. Please feel free to make as many copies as necessary for your personal use.

4 Factors (4 "I's")

The 4 Factors Worksheet consist of a master worksheet, and 4 subsets of worksheets that will assist you to create an overall plan of action. These subset worksheets are: Basic Values Worksheet, Vision Statement Worksheet, Mission Statement Worksheet, and SMART Target Goal Setting. Once you have completed the subsets, you will complete the Master Worksheet in order to have all of the information in one place for reference.

Remember that you also have access to an entire training on BASIC VALUES available as a bonus for purchasing this book. You can access that at http://donnawoolam.com/confidentleader/cv-bonus

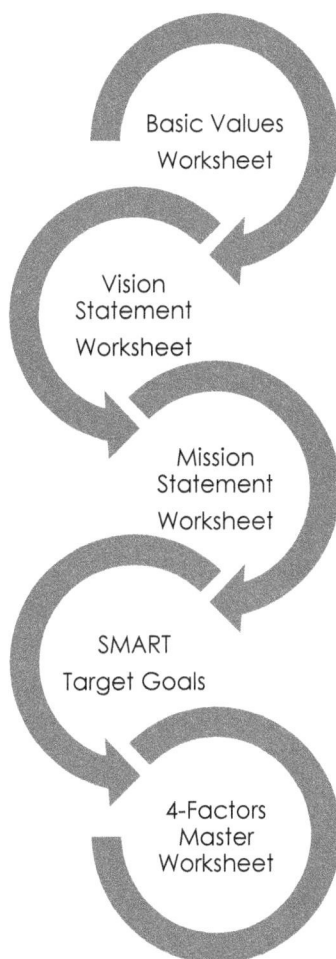

Basic Values
Worksheet

Vision
Statement
Worksheet

Mission
Statement
Worksheet

SMART
Target Goals

4-Factors
Master
Worksheet

Basic Values Worksheet

You have many values that influence and color your everyday life. In the space below, write freely about all of the things that are important to you, both personally and in your business life.

From the sentences above, select 7-10 Basic Value WORDS and write them below. For instance: honesty, safety, fun, etc.

List 7-10 Basic Values that are the **MOST IMPORTANT** to you.

1 _____

2 _____

3 _____

4 _____

5 _____

6 _____

7 _____

8 _____

9 _____

10 _____

In the following section, **MORE CLEARLY DEFINE** each word. That is, create a statement about each word, and the motivational/emotional factor from which it comes. You can review these below the worksheet. Remember that **VALUES** are based on emotions, not goals. If you say, *the best*, what is the emotional value of that term; is it pride in accomplishment; satisfaction of achievement, etc.? List them in their order of importance. Note whether they fall into the areas of **INTENTION, INFORMATION, INTERACTION** or **INFLUENCE**.

Basic Value Word	Definition	Application

By this point, you have defined the top 7-10 Basic Value statements that you believe are important, both to you as a leader, and to your organization's success. If you are still unclear about how these Basic Values will work within your organization, take some time to think about how your team will look when the Values you have listed are implemented. If something doesn't "fit" you may need to re-evaluate its place within the organization as a whole.

If it doesn't fit into one of the **4 I's**, you will also want to consider the motivational/emotional connection to the value to see if you need a different motivational/emotional definition attached to the word itself.

From *Design Your Culture, Empower Your Team*

No matter where I researched, there are **10 Primary Values** that are common to mankind. Within each of these values, you have created an opinion of what is, and isn't, acceptable, reasonable, and appropriate for the environment in which you find yourself. Each one of these 10 basic values falls within the first *FOUR I's* of the *Thinking From the End* system that you are learning in this book: **INTENTION, INFORMATION, INTERACTION, and INFLUENCE.** They can be characterized by describing the central *motivational* goal.

Independent Thought and Action

Excitement, Novelty and Challenge

Pleasure and Gratification

Personal Success

Power

Security

Conformity

Tradition

Benevolence

Inclusiveness

Somewhere within these 10 tenets, you will discover the truths that are most important to you as a leader and how you will lead your group, team or organization.

Craft Your Vision Statement Worksheet

Your Vision Statement will become a, short, concise, and inspirational document for the members of the group. It provides a central point, a north star, for the group to focus its efforts. Your goal is to engage the group with what is possible within the organization. The Vision Statement declares, **"When all things are working perfectly, THIS will happen!"** *– Quote from Design Your Culture ~ Empower Your Team*

Write **FREELY** (don't try to make it pretty), all that you would like to see within your organization. From these sentences, we will bring your thoughts down to one or two sentences that clearly state what you intend.

NOW, hone in on what you want to say, **EXACTLY.** Use the back of this worksheet to play around with wording and phrasing. You'll want to move words around until you have designed a meaningful statement with content that:

    1) looks to the future;
    2) elicits an emotional response;
    3) acts as the cornerstone for future activity;
    4) declares what the "best end result" looks like; and,
    5) is to the point.

In the space below, write out your completed Vision Statement.

Craft Your Mission Statement Worksheet

Now is your opportunity to begin to fully declare and breathe life into your Vision Statement. Whereas your Vision Statement is a short, concise statement, your Mission Statement, is something that can be sung or shouted from the rooftops!

There are four questions to ask in order to design a great Mission Statement. They are:

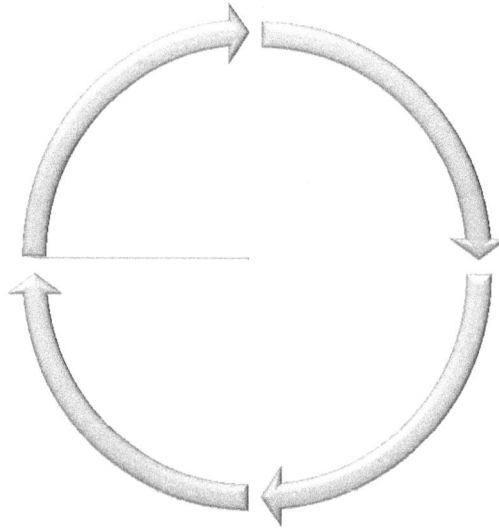

What do we do? _____

_____

_____

How do we do it? _____

_____

_____

Whom do we do it for? _____

_____

_____

What value are we bringing? (Or, Why?) _____

_____

_____

Now that you have answered the four questions, you should be able to write out your Mission Statement. Take some time with this. Think about the words and the emotion they invoke. Do they inspire and motivate, as well as give information?

Target Goal Setting Worksheet

My preferred method of setting goals is called **TARGET GOAL SETTING**. Simply put, it means that anywhere within the TARGET is a win! It may not be the bull's eye, but you still get points for hitting the target itself.

As part of the **Thinking from the End** point of view, Target Goal Setting is a basic system to "**I'll Do This or Else**" (anywhere within the target) and the "**This is the BEST Result**" (bull's eye) accomplishment. We call these ACCEPTABLE Results and BULL'S EYE Results.

You will create a Target Goal for **each** of your Mission Statement sentences of: **What do we do? How do we do it? Whom do we do it for? What value are we bringing (or WHY)?**

As you begin to work through the Goals, you will develop goals within them. Be sure to complete a Target Goal Sheet for each step.

As you work through the steps of **Information, Interaction and Influence**, you will fill in more answers. By the end of the workbook, you will have created the final step of **Implementation**.

Remember that the acrostic we are using is **S.M.A.R.T.** Every goal that you create must be:

> **Specific**
> **Measureable**
> **Attainable**
> **Results-Oriented**
> **Time Bound**

You will ask several questions along the way as you are creating your Target Goal Sheets. Some of them are:

1. What are the steps to get to the end?
2. What are the tools, services, etc. needed to take the steps?
3. Who will oversee the activity?
4. Where will this take place?
5. What is the deadline for it to be accomplished?
6. What is my Bull's Eye Result?
7. What is my Target Result?

SMART Target Goals Worksheet
Specific | Measurable | Action-Oriented | Realistic | Time Bound

What is the specific goal?_____

What is the Acceptable Result? _____

What is the Bull's Eye Result? _____

Why is this goal important to achieve?_____

_____

Where does it fit in the *Four I's*? Intention ____ Information ____ Interaction ____ Influence ____

Who will oversee the completion of this goal? _____

What criteria proves this goal is attainable? _____

_____

What steps are required in order to realize the goal? _____

_____

What resources are needed? _____

_____

When will progress be checked? (Daily, weekly, monthly?) _____

_____

What barriers will/can prevent achievement of the goal? _____

_____

How will barriers be addressed? _____

_____

What results will be in evidence when the goal is accomplished? _____

_____

What is the time frame to reach this goal? _____

_____

What must be done each day to achieve the goal? _____

_____

INFORMATION

The Information section of your Resource Workbook provides you with a tool to keep track of how you are delivering information to your team.

Information Flow Chart

Use this chart when you are preparing training, information or data for your organization. This will ensure that you are providing information in various formats in order to meet the needs of your entire organization. There is no need to use all forms all the time, but having a track record will assist you in identifying solutions should issues arise.

Project Name: _____

Type of Information: _____

Purpose of Information: _____

Length of Information: _____

How Will the Information be Relayed (Live, Recorded, Written)? _____

Who is Providing Information? _____

Auditory Tools to Use: _____

Visual Tools to Use: _____

Kinesthetic Tools to Use: _____

INTERACTION

Basic Group Meeting Agenda

Date | Time _____ *| Location* _____

Meeting called by		Attendees
Type of meeting		
Facilitator		Please read
Note taker		
Timekeeper		Please bring

Agenda Items

Topic	Presenter	Time allotted
☐		
☐		
☐		
☐		
☐		
☐		
☐		

OTHER INFORMATION

Observers

Resources

Special notes

INFLUENCE

Influence Your World Worksheet

> *There are many avenues of Influence. Your organization will have to determine how much it wants to extend outside of itself to work with other organizations, groups, or entities. The form below is simply a tool to assist the organization in making the best use of its time and resources.*

How can we use what we have learned to assist someone else? _____

_____

What unique skills, gifts or talents do we possess? _____

_____

_____

Should we designate an individual or group to bring needs to our attention? _____

_____

Is there an organization outside our company that could benefit from our experience? _____

_____

Is there an organization within our company that could benefit from our experience? _____

_____

Is there an individual who could benefit from our assistance? _____

_____

Is there a charitable organization we are drawn to assist? _____

_____

Is there a project our company is promoting which we could support? _____

_____

What resources do we have which we could share? _____

_____

What resources are no longer needed that could be donated? _____

_____

INTERRUPTION

Interruption Worksheet

Something isn't working. It may be PERSONAL, PROCESS, or PEOPLE issues. The following empowering questions will assist you in not only identifying the areas of Interruption, but hopefully provide answers for resolution as well.

Empowering Questions for Yourself

1) Have YOU lost your passion for the group, team, organization or project?

2) Are you confident in yourself as a leader?

3) Are you overbearing?

4) Are you consistent?

5) Are you trustworthy?

6) Are you generous with praise for the efforts of the other team members?

7) Do you reserve judgment and criticism for private meetings?

8) Are you attending meetings, or seeking out education and information that will strengthen your leadership skills?

9) Have you sought out a mentor or personal coach?

10) Are you willing to be wrong? Do you take criticism gracefully and with an ear to hear the truth?

11) Are you approachable?

Empowering Questions for the Process

1) Are you clear about the Vision?

2) Is the Mission Statement practical?

3) Have you created SMART Goals - Specific, Measurable, Attainable, Results-Oriented, Time-Bound?

4) Is the training that is needed in place?

5) Have you established an environment of mutual respect?

6) Are achievers of specific goals being recognized?

7) Does your group have a way to give back or extend its influence?

8) Is there an outside person that can come and speak to your group in order to give them a boost?

9) Can the group work in a different location?

Empowering Questions for the Team

1) If you HAVE NOT YET implemented these Systems, ask yourself who in your present group you anticipate being resistant. Is there a way to bring them on board the planning committee to discuss your Vision for the team?

2) If you HAVE ALREADY BEGUN to implement these Systems, and are meeting resistance, is there a way to bring the dissenter(s) into the process?

3) Have you clearly presented the information in a variety of ways? Perhaps your dissenter(s) are missing a Basic element in understanding because the information is not being presented in their primary learning style.

4) Do you need to have a one-on-one conversation? Questions you can ask in the conversation:

1. What do you really want?
2. How can I help right now?
3. If you had a choice what would you do?
4. What gets in your way in this area?
5. Can you delegate that?
6. How could you simplify that?
7. What goal are you ready to achieve?
8. What skill do you most want to learn?
9. What gifts aren't being fully developed?
10. What is your most important project?

5) After hearing their concerns, is it possible to come to a mutual agreement?

6) If you cannot come to a mutual agreement for adjustment, it is important for them to understand why you are unable or unwilling to make a shift in the process.

IMPLEMENTATION
Declaration of Worth

What is your **WOW**; your **WITHIN ONE WEEK** plan? I have a Declaration Statement for you. Learn it, print it out, frame it. Every week, complete a **WOW Card** to keep yourself on track with your goals.

I am a Woman of Worth.
Not because of what I do or don't do,
but because of who I am.
I am a Woman.
My confidence is not that I am perfect;
that is, a woman without flaws.
My confidence is that I am a woman of
excellence; that is, a woman of distinction.
As I walk my life's journey, I commit to
being a woman who opens doors of
opportunities for others, and assists
them on their journey to
Confident, Inspired Living.

W.O.W. Cards (Within One Week)

W.O.W.
My **Within One Week** Commitment is:

W.O.W.
My **Within One Week** Commitment is:

Last Thoughts

As a woman in business, I have struggled to find answers that worked for me and my situation.

I would often find something that ALMOST fit. The result is that I took what I could find and changed it to fit my circumstances. That's what you find here. You may have seen some tools here that are similar to tools you've investigated. That wouldn't surprise me at all, because most systems are built around the same core strategies. I've done my best not to plagiarize, nor cannibalize my fellow leadership trainers. Every document is unique to me. Because I have studied a vast amount of knowledge, there is bound to be some spillage.

I do hope that you have discovered new items for your Leadership Tool Box. Perhaps my "tweak here, tweak there" is just what YOU need for your organization.

Please remember that what you have here are only the resources, the training that goes along with them is very important and found within the book ***Design Your Culture, Empower Your Team.***

I have a favor to ask, will you email me your thoughts about this workbook? I would like to know how to make it better. My email is donna@donnawoolam.com.

Also, if you plan to share this workbook, please share the book with them as well. The bookstore link for this series is http://livingatmybest.com .

As always,

Live At Your Best ~ Live Inspired,

Donna

What Next?

The ability to believe in your own greatness will greatly determine whether or not you move forward. Often, even when we want to believe something is truth, we can get stuck in old patterns of thinking. We can't seem to make the step from knowing the truth, into believing the truth. And if you can't believe it, you can't live it.

This is when a little help can empower us to make that critical step. In my life, this has been the place where a coach has made the difference.

A coach is not necessarily a psychologist, a doctor, nor a licensed therapist. A coach is someone who walks with you through a process to develop skills and confidence. A coach reminds me of Glinda the Good Witch of the Wizard of Oz. She tells Dorothy, "My dear, you had the power to go home within you all along."

A good coach will not tell you WHAT to do, but will help you to recognize and draw out the power that is within you to make the changes you desire.

There are many types of coaches; from life, to business development, to health or executive leadership. Depending on the changes you want to see implemented in your life, you have your choice of a never-ending supply of people whose one aim is to help you achieve your goals.

A coach is invested in your success, and has compassion on your situations, but doesn't become co-dependent with you in the circumstances. In other words, your coach holds you accountable for the decisions and actions you make, or don't make.

Not only have I had the benefit of having a coach, I have the privilege of being a coach. I've worked with women of all ages and backgrounds navigate both life issues, and business building strategies.

I'd like to offer you the opportunity to have a free thirty minute coaching session with me. During that time, we can discuss some of the areas you might feel a bit stuck. After the complimentary session, we can discuss whether you believe you could benefit from continuing in a paid coaching relationship with me.

Along with my elite program of private, one-on-one coaching, I offer focused group coaching, which includes partnering with others on the same goal path; group coaching for your organization to address relationship or business building skills; and, regular teleseminars and webinars.

Additionally, I am available to speak and train to groups, large and small, on subjects that pertain to women and their lives and business.

No matter which of these will benefit you, know that I am committed to working with you to help bring YOUR goals to life. You have a God-ordained destiny. I would be honored to be His vessel to walk beside you on the road to the realization of your dreams and visions.

You can learn more about available programs at http://donnawoolam.com/coaching.

Connect With Donna

LIKE my PAGE on Facebook: http://facebook.com/TheLifeInspired

FOLLOW me on Twitter: http://twitter.com/donnakwoolam

CONNECT on LinkedIn: http://linkedin.com/in/donnawoolam

Join My Online Community: http://donnawoolam.com

Are you in need of a speaker for your group or program?
Please contact me at 214.463.7995 or through my website. Or email me at
donna@donnawoolam.com.

Other Books by Donna K Woolam

Available at http://LivingAtMyBest.com

Breathtaking! Discover and Release Your Greatness

LEARN ABOUT OTHER BOOKS IN THE
Confident, Inspired Woman ~ Leadership Series

http://donnawoolam.com/ConfidentLeader

Upcoming Titles:

Coaching for Success: Empower Others & Change Lives

You Can Be a Great Leader: Legacy Leadership - Empowering Others to Become Great Leaders